CRUMBS III

Feed The Poet Within

CANDACE R. BAILLY

Camesa Publishing LLC

Candace R. Bailly

☙❦❧

First Edition December 2021

ASIN (eBook)

ISBN (Print) 978-1-953514-00-4

Published by Camesa Publishing LLC

Www.CamesaPublishing.com

☙❦❧

Dedicated to you my family. I love you.

INTRODUCTION

These poems range from haiku to free verse; note, the free verse is wildly-wild free-form. As you browse the pages, you'll notice the poems are co-mingled in style but split by categories (e.g., Love, Not Always (love), You, Me, Writing, and Nature). This setup allows you to jump around to find the poems that fit your mood.

In these poems, you'll find the dreamer, the romantic, the wishful thinker, the child, the pessimist, and sometimes the fool...which is to say, 'another human trying to make sense of this crazy world.' Ok, so that's everything you need to know, so jump in and happy reading.

ALWAYS LOVE

L ove with your whole heart,
love without expectations,
give it all you have...

MY HEAD IS SWIMMING,
that woozy, heavy feeling
any time you're near.

WE LAY TOGETHER,
folded forms, twisted, tangled:
never happier.

COME SIT on my lap
curl into a cat-like ball

and I'll caress you.

❦

RAGING like bonfires
      flames flicking high, lapping air,
      leaving embers on.

❦

We met amidst smoke
      and set the bonfire ablaze,
      now rest mid embers.

❦

ON HOT SUMMER nights
      dancing under moonlit skies,
      alone-time with you.

❦

DAY in and day out
      sitting alone, waiting here
      hoping there'll be more.

❦

ALL I DO IS WAIT
      wondering where I fit in,
      knowing it's nowhere.

❦

IF YOU CAN'T FIND me,
　　know that I'm by the water
　　to dream of us.

❧

TELL HOW YOU LOVE ME,
　　for the road was not taken
　　I wander alone.

❧

BLOOMS OPEN, stretch high
　　letting rays caress and bathe
　　but then—weed whacker!

❧

THERE WAS a time when
　　nothing else mattered but us
　　but — reality.

❧

IT'S THE LOOK, the feel
　　of intense, pure passion,
　　total commitment.

❧

YOU LOOKED STRAIGHT AT ME,
　　so I froze and stopped breathing,
　　then you said my name.

❦

THAT FEELING you have
 when you first wake up and know
 our world is perfect.

❦

WHEN WE'RE TOGETHER
 I strive for only one state:
 pure satisfaction.

❦

WE SWAM WITH DOLPHINS,
 played in the blue ocean, and
 sang the siren song.

AT NIGHT, we rested
 under the moon-lit black skies
 to dream all the dreams.

WHEN THE DOLPHINS left
 and a new sun had risen,
 we were still dreamin'.

❦

A LONG TIME ago
 I held your hand while we walked.
 The path was endless.

✤

WHEN I CLOSE my eyes
  I see your smile, feel your touch.
  Please let it be real.

✤

HOW DO you keep love
  when it can ghost through you and
  onto the next one?.

✤

PRESSED flowers in books
  to hang onto memories
  of special moments.

✤

WHEN I TAKE A STROLL,
  I dream of love...loyalty,
  then doubt where it lives.

✤

HEAR THE DRUMS...CONSTANT:
  Beating, pounding, thumping on.
  Thy soul vibrates...deep.

NOT ALWAYS

Blank face stared at me.
    There was nothing left to say.
    We knew—it was done.

❧

FROM DARKNESS, she rose.
    And engulfed the world in flames.
    Her fierceness revealed.

❧

MY WORDS SLIDE WITH WINDS,
    whispering their way through fields
    but fall on deaf ears.

❧

GETTING in is all

that matters; getting out is
for the fun of it.

❦

WHEN YOU READ THESE WORDS,
    do you think they're about you?
    If you answer yes... .

❦

SHE SAID the right things
    and presented herself well,
    but stole all he had.

❦

HE SPOKE only facts
    but riddled with opinions
    and thought he was right.

❦

KNOW "BUTTONS MCGEE"?
    He gets all wound up when you
    press certain topics.

❦

YOU DON'T KNOW the facts
    and shamelessly felt compelled
    to comment and judge.

❦

WHAT ONCE WE held dear
    slipped through our fevered embrace:
    the fleeting passions.

FOR YOU

T he bed warm, cozy;
         after a night of drinking,
         we we woke naked.

HANDS GRIP thy throat tight
    leaving the body limp while
    the color drains out...

WHAT IS LEFT behind
    is not for your gentle heart.
    Turn now, do not look.

FRACK YA'LL, I'm still here!
    Now I'm doing life my way.

Butterfly wings flap.

❧

SHE BRAVELY WALKED IN;
    they beat her down...and again.
    But stood tall, she did.

❧

PATHS TAKEN when young
    are met with eagerness, but
    life will change that path.

❧

FIGHT for what's right
    with a full heart and strong hands:
    Honor will prevail.

❧

WHETHER TO PONDER
    or self reflect, this is the
    relaxed position.

❧

DEMONS live in minds
    and haunt us endlessly if
    they stay in control.

❧

THE HAUNTING hour wakes
   bringing out ghouls to steal our
   souls and behead us.

❧

FOREVER FOCUSED:
   strength is my one salvation.
   I am best right here.

❧

HONORABLE LIFE
   spent building and supporting
   the collective good.

❧

YOU'RE SO fierce and strong.
   But inner peace only comes
   when you prove yourself.

❧

ECLIPSE

THE MOON
   claims its due!

Darkness
   Isn't forever

.   .   .

ENCOMPASSED
   By light

※

DELIVER me from
   all human inflicted pains;
   set me free, I'll rise.

※

THE COOL CAT STROLLED IN,
   so into self, she snubbed all
   and was left alone.

※

WAKING every day
   and sharing it with loved ones
   is a dream come true.

※

BLOOD PRESSURE RISES,
   the heartbeat becomes rapid
   and clear thinking stalls.

※

I'M ALWAYS anxious
   and it's for no good reason,
   I remind myself.

※

You see a young girl
    being defiant or smug.
    I see our future.

[This haiku was written in 2017 and dedicated to women around the world for the #MeToo & #StrongerTogether movements.]

☙

YOUR TRUTH

Don't be afraid
    to be disruptive
    because you'll live
    more fully.

You'll live freely,
    and feel completely...
    Live a truth
    NO

Live your truth,
    Be alive
    Be Free
    Be you!

☙

WHERE DOES your mind go
when you leave here and now?
Are you still present?

JUST ME

Aroma alone
　　fills my senses, but first sip...
　　"Ahhh" the day begins.

[DEDICATED TO COFFEE. Yes, you read that correctly...I love coffee, especially a pour-over.]

❧

MASK

WHEN I AM ALONE,
　　I mean complete solitude,
　　There is no mask, none.

I'M HERE, I am me.

But if someone comes close, well,
The magic mask donned.

THE ROLES HAVE BEEN SET,
      And there's nothing I can do
      But hide behind it.

❦

I HAVE WHAT I HAVE;
      No more, no less, it's just right
      because it is true.

❦

REMEMBER those days
      Filled with dreams, hopes, and passions;
      I long for those days.

❦

SELF DEPRECATING...
      I'm stuck inside my own head,
      get me out of here!

❦

NEVER ENDING NOISE!
      If I responded out loud,
      I would say "Shut up!"

❦

MY HEART IS deep red
    but my soul is vibrant blues
    and lives in the seas.

❧

I LIVE IN MY DREAMS:
    It's where I'm happiest and
    no one can change it.

❧

WE CHOOSE our own brush
    to make colors swirl and flow:
    painting life to see.

❧

"WEIRD" is happening
    And I'm not sure what or why.
    But my bones feel it.

❧

WRECKED

THE SHIP CRASHES
    through the waves
    in the storm.

IT CRASHES through wave after wave
    until the hull gives way.

. . .

WATER RUSHES IN
    filling each cabin
    with dark waters.

SEA-SALT FINDS its way
    into every crevice and
    wound of the ship.

THE SHIP LISTS
    heavily to one side,
    fighting to stay upright.

BUT WITH THE bow pointed to the heavens,
    and the weight of the water inside,
    the ship loses purchase and sinks.

Glub-glubbing,
    planks cracking,
    all the way down.

THE SAND IS SPLIT APART
    in total darkness, as the ship
    bangs, cracks, and glubs in disbelief.

IT UNWILLINGLY SETTLES
    into its new existence,

waiting for the next storm.

ALL THE STORMS or any storm,
    But that will never, ever
    reach this one again.

[THIS IS A REWRITE of my 2017 Wrecked.]

෴

DEMOLITION

I'M NOT what you believe me to be,
    I'm not what I think I am.

FOR THAT MATTER, not even what I wish to be.
    I am, however, a ball of anxious energy.

I WANT to be better than I am, of course.
    Now, if only that could be.

UNFORTUNATELY, the answer is no
    because I am... this, just this.

ASK anyone who knows me
    they will confirm, I'm just me.

                                    .   .   .

I SHAN'T apologize again and again.
So move along, there is no more.

FOUND

I'M NOT IMPORTANT.
And
I'm not "all that."

IT WAS difficult to learn this. True.
Because
I thought I was or should be "more."

THERE IS zero pressure from the 'masses'.
Now.
I am just one voice.

BUT IT IS MY VOICE.
Mine.
Now that I'm not trying to be 'all that.'

I SPEAK UP; I speak my mind.
Aloud.
It's my voice. And I find I like it very much.

HEAR ME? Don't hear me?

No matter,
I'll pour myself into life and live free.

I AM MINE AGAIN.
    I am me.
    And this is my voice.

5

ABOUT WRITING

I think about words
    because they're how we create
    a life with meaning.

❦

SPACING, meter, tone;
    Reveals all you need to know
    When it's needed most.

❦

"MENTOR, I found you!
    Wait, let me get a notepad." ...
    "Who the hell are you?"

❦

HOW SHOULD I BEHAVE?
    What should a I say and to whom?

Where's the portal out?

❧

ALL THE WORDS I write
 are alone and full of dread
 but then light creeps in.

❧

FEELINGS SWIM, words fly
 And ideas float in space:
 get grounded and write.

❧

WAKE UP, drink coffee,
 then get refills all day long,
 "Please, caffè latte" .

6

TO NATURE

Black widow creeps in
    Unnoticed; she moves in close
    hoping to end him.

❀

HOUSES DONNED merry
    with the pristine white attire
    to glisten and glow.

❀

GALAXY WAS BORN:
    From the very beginning
    we're destined to BE.

❀

OPEN YOUR EYES—SEE!
    The autumn leaves and blue skies

bring distant rain storms.

❦

EACH YEAR, flowers bloomed,
    leaves changed colors, and snow fell.
    But I stayed the same.

❦

PEOPLE SUNBATHING
    while ice-cold waves crash shorelines
    and searing rays bake.

❦

IT FEELS soft and glides
    to the ground where snow piles, and
    crunches underfoot.

❦

BANANAS ARE ripe
    apples and oranges are firm,
    oh, but the cherries!

❦

COLD HARSH LANDSCAPE, gone!
    I want to lay in the grass
    And feel the warm breeze.

MORE CRUMBS

& YOUR INVITATION

You've finished CRuMBs Chapbook III, the third book in the CRuMBs series! The next (and final) chapbook in the series is scheduled to be released in 2022. Follow Candace's blog to keep in touch and get updates. (The social links are shown on the *About the Author* page.)

The best way to find out about upcoming release dates is via the free Newsletter.

Join us here:
www.CandyH2O.com/subscribe

REVIEW

Thank you for reading this book! Please leave a review because this helps a great deal. For your convenience, the link to the *Author Page* where you can review this book is shown below:

Amazon.com/author/candacemisnerbailly

৩৯৩

EPILOGUE

I hope you enjoyed the book because I thoroughly enjoyed writing it! My poetry is weird for some people, I know, but my hope is that you found some poems that resonated within you. Either way, thank you for reading and best wishes. Also, if you enjoyed my weird brain shenanigans, be sure to find me on social media (the links are shared on the *About the Author* page).

ALSO BY CANDACE R. BAILLY

Find all of CR Bailly's published works at:
Www.CandyH2O.com/Works

CRuMBs I & II - Feed The Poet Within
Available now

The Addicted
First time published: 2014, Romance Magazine Vol. 02, No. 06.
Second time published: 2019, CRuMBs I.

It's In The Cards
Co-authored

Masters of Networking
Contributing Author

❧

ABOUT THE AUTHOR

Candace grew up in California and earned a Bachelor of Science in Business. In the middle of her studies, she took a break to serve her country: US Naval Intelligence, Pentagon, Washington DC. Following her service, she married and raised two daughters. Candace currently lives in the Northwest. As of late, she spends her days researching, writing, editing, and publishing new material.

Candace also sketches and paints (watercolors). Some of these works get posted to the blog. Check it out.

Keep in touch:
Blog: candyh2o.com/blog
Twitter: twitter.com/candyh2o
Pinterest: pinterest.com/candyh2o
GoodReads: goodreads.com/candacebailly
Amazon Author:
amazon.com/author/candacemisnerbailly